# Table of Contents

# Chapter One

# Aandem Aaki

## Vocabulary Preview

1. **Dexterous**--- skillful
2. **Prevaricate**--- To avert, to put off
3. **Epilogue**--- A short conclusion.
4. **Ersatz**-- Artificial, fake.

# Chapter One

# Aandem Aaki

There was a man who lived in a village. He was called Aandem Aaki. He was a **dexterous** hunter who never came home without game. He never missed his target. His enemies knew that attacking him or his friends will bring him out. Aandem Aaki lost his parents when he was 17. By then he had mastered the art of hunting. He chased pythons for pepper soup and fought with lions and leopards for the forest kingship. He despised cutting-grass and porcupine as game for women. When other hunters who were older than him jubilated bringing home squirrels and ratmoles, he will grind in bemusement that any man, talk less of a hunter should be happy with such an achievement. He was young but when the time for truth came, he never **prevaricated**. He was brave and courageous in the face of evil.

As his skills grew, his popularity increased. They called him all sorts of titles; nkwo mmu (real man), nnemen-nok (iroko), ekrisu bhaghosong (mirror if young girls), nyah na aanen (bitter meat), moh Mmandem (child of God), eronghoh etok (light of the town) and others called him in direct titles papa, daddy, mfor (chief) etaahyeseh (our father). Indeed he was all of that. When he passed, young girls ran to their doors to see and smile with him. If he wanted to marry, he would have done that in a heartbeat. On the market day, the bevies of young girls and galaxies of women seemed to be waiting just for a word. He was the mirror women used to look at themselves. If he told anyone of them that she was beautiful, she might not take a shower again because the very reason to prove herself beautiful has endorsed her already. He was jocund and full of largess to them.

The men who were jealous of him ensnared him, but he will never fall. They talked evil of him and said he has bought powers from the underworld, others said that he had joined a secret society, and some said he had sold part of his body to be popular. It was none of that! He drank the poison that old men gave without realizing he drank poison because it would seem God was with him. One day he felt on the same trap he had set for an antelope. The trap took him and slammed him on the trunk of a mahogany that was just by the side because that is the way the trapped worked. It slammed the antelope's back on the tree to break its spinal cord. Yet, Aandem Aaki came out unscathed. His fame went beyond the villages and reechoed to visiting strangers.

When people attacked his friend, they knew they were in for war. Aandem Aaki will never start a war, but he ended it at his timing. He was dexterous, he knew which arrow to shoot, he knew which trap to set, and he knew the weaknesses of all his enemies. He won all his wrestling matches in the village as he constantly slipped off the attempted chokes of his adversaries. Even animals had learned to avoid his territory because he was a conqueror.

Despite all of that, he was a man of the people. He helped the widows and widowers, orphans and weeping parents in the village. He accompanied young people to the stream to fetch water. If he was passing and saw any woman trying to split firewood, Aandem Aaki will stop to split it for her. He went and broke melons with total strangers. When someone died, he will spend the night there. He will always come with palmwine and some game for them to drink and cook for the mourners. You could see why they called him eronghoh etok or why others went the distance to call him moh Mmandem. He had qualities that made life easier for others even though he had never set foot in church.

There was not a villager who did not know Aandam Aaki. The surrounding villages had heard of his good works. Parents began naming their kids Aandam Aaki. At 22, it was

4

difficult to know the real Aandem Aaki because anyone with the name became instantly popular and famous. There you could see that it is failure that is always alone; success always has brothers and sisters, some he does not even know.

Then the lights went off! Aandem Aaki died in his sleep. **Epilogue** has it that the ancestors took him for breaking a law, but others argued that he took all the glory of his talents and skills for himself rather than give the glory to God. Still some said he died of slow poison. Some Christians said God does not allow real good people to live long. I don't know which one to believe, but I know that we all missed him. You know that many people had died in the village without anyone missing them. But the village mourned Aandem Aaki for more than seven conservative days. At last the light was extinguished! "Oh Aandem" the young girls mourned. The dotards said "nnemenok adese bhioreh" the great tree has absconded majestically. The same life that no mortal, no spirit visible or invisible could conquer is put out without any struggle and very young.

Nevertheless, young people grew old but still remember Aandem Aaki. Aandem Aaki is gone leaving behind his **ersatz.** "Oh Aandem Aaki, you made life easier for us." It was not for nothing, it was not by coincidence, but it seems by divine ordination that his parents gave him that name Aandem Aaki. Literally it means ho who say what he does. It simply means a man who keeps his promises. In American parlance they say "he walks the talk." When you keep your promises to God and man, you will be missed if you died no matter the age. So would people miss you if you died today? Are you harnessing the skills in your young children? Is the community glad to see you?

Until then, be an Aandem Aaki.

# Chapter Two

# Mispah

## Vocabulary Preview

1. **Nexus**—A connection point.

# Chapter Two

# MISPAH

I had written about this dog before in one of my articles, but as I was traveling, I saw a couple that looked more like strangers to themselves than couples. Then I narrated this story I am telling you now. At the end of the story, the woman sobbed as the man kissed her over and over. There was a couple Mr. & Mrs. Nenfackkitoyi that inherited a dog from a shelter. Surely the previous owner had given it a name, but when the dog came to their house, they gave it a new name- Mispah. The woman was the one who brought the dog, but the dog forced its love on the husband. At this time, their marriage was on the rocks. The dog indeed was going to live its name.

When each parent came back from work, it greeted them in their turns and saw them off as they left. Many times, they left home together, and Mispah walked on the left and later walked on the right trying to show her allegiance and love to both. The parents fell it was their only **nexus** to reconciliation as their eyes joined each time they tried to look at the dog. Soon they began teaming up to play with the dog, and consequently the glow of their tattered marriage was burning with new steam.

Mispah was permitted to hunt. When she brought game, she kept it on the floor in front of the father. Then she will carry it latter to the mother and then to the father front and back until the father will seize the porcupine from her mouth and give it to the wife to cook.

When they were eating, Mispah ate in her plate but attempted several times to eat from the plate of Mr. & Mrs. Nenfackkitoyi. When one parent pushed her off, she will go to the next parent. If the father pushed her off, she went to the mother.

One day, they were to go on vacation; they gathered their things and prepared the dog's house and left her with enough food and drinks. She has grown to serve herself and to hunt for food when she was hungry; however, she was not prepared to deal with the absence of Mr. & Mrs. Nenfackkitoyi she sacrificially loved.

As they left the house, she walked as usual; changing positions, kissing the mother and kissing the father. Then they each took their different directions. Mispah will run and kiss Mrs. Nenfackkitoyi , and then runs back to kiss Mr. Nenfackkitoyi. With time, the gap between both parents increased, and Mispah's trips too increased. She had just kissed the father and was running to kiss the mother when a car came from the side and hit her unto the pavement. With her parents gone, and in a country where dogs are not cared for, she bled with groans of love by the corner of the road for her parents until her sun set. More so, she died in the absence of her beloved who could give her a befitting burial.

No matter how great our love is, we cannot serve two masters at a time. Some people say that it was because of love that she died, but others says it was because of greed because she wanted to love the two parents the same way at the same time. Others conclude that whatever the case, the conclusion is that Mispah died loving her parents.

Will we say that you love your parents if you were to die today? Would anyone say you loved them unto death if you were to die today? How is your love; when there is no money? Is your love only in good times? Do those who love you sleep with you as a sheep sleeps with a lion? In the perfect world, the lion and the sheep will sleep together, but in this present world, though the lion and the sheep may sleep together the sheep would not have much sleep. Mispah is dead, but she left a lesson for us to learn: unconditional and everlasting love until death do you part.

Until then, be ready to die for those you love.

# Chapter Three

# Papa Elephant

## Vocabulary Preview

1. **Manacles**—Strong iron chains to restrain people or animals.
2. **Encroaching**—Advance beyond boundaries or limits.

# Chapter Three

# Papa Elephant

He was a prosperous child of a man popularly known as Papa Africa who had 53 children. Africa and all his children were doing well. They lived peacefully with one another and helped each other overcome those natural and man-made disasters. Across the water lived a popular Master thief called Yankee. That was good news to Yankee. His father was a Christian but he had backslidden.

Around 1492, Master Thief sent his grandkids to steal the grand kids of Africa. They took them to their village where they put them in shackles and **manacles** and forced them to work for free for more than 200 years. They went and hid them in other villages so they will be working for them. After some time, some of Yankee's grandkids revolted and said they did not more want to steal other human beings especially the children of Papa Africa.

During this time, the cousin of Yankee called Diana who lived in a small Island by herself had become an armed robber too. Rumor has it that thievery was a curse in their family, for they are cursed to steal only other human beings. She gathered her friends Marianne, Leopold, Charles, and Bismarck and they decided to go and live in Papa Africa's village without his permission so that they will steal things to their own country and then change the village heads there. That was short-lived as the grandkids of Papa Africa drove them out after some time. Almost all have left except Marianne and Charles.

One of Papa Africa's child- Papa Elephant decided to settle in the West where he shared boundary with a mysterious water called Atlantic and five of his other brothers- Lone Stars,

Syli Nationale, Aigles, Etalons and Wagadugu. Their father had a lot of land, cattle and natural resources like gold, oil, bauxite, elephants and diamonds that made Master Thief, Marianne and Diana spend sleepless nights. They colluded to steal those resources.

The boy was getting prosperous, so he decided to join a little brotherhood group called ECOWAS. Little did he know these were turncoats to whom he has sold his soul. They survived by drinking the blood of their brothers. They began by **encroaching** into his land because he was an orphan.

Yankee was now using his cousin Diana as a lapdog. Diana too has made Yankee's friend-Marianne her lappuppy. One day Diana entreated Yankee and promised him goodies from the exploit if they will kidnap Papa Elephant's brother Warriors. Unfortunately, though the man was still young, he had a son in his early age called Bob. He fought them with his might and age until they left him alone.

Meanwhile, Marianne had heard that Papa Elephant had some two rebel sons called Soro and Quattara. So she supplied them with weapons and ammunitions so that they will rob their own father. Unfortunately for them, their father had a faithful son called Gbagbo. Gbagbo fought them until they retreated back to Etalons and Syli Nationale. Etalons had a very bad son who killed his own childhood friend just so he will replace him as head of the village. Everyone knew Compaore to be very mean spirited. When Marianne heard of everything that was happening to the old men in these villages, she decided to solicit the help of the notorious gang called the UN. This gang is known for kidnapping and raping the male children of the old man with a bent back called Papa Africa.

The UN called the Brotherhood –ECOWAS led by Badluck, and they planned a massive thievery through elections. When that did not work, they then decided that they will steal the old man by force. They began saying that they want to kidnap Papa Elephant because his son Gbagbo has stolen the title of family head. Everyone knew that the gang, master thief, and especially Marianne only want all the utensils in Papa Elephant's house. "Having they stolen enough?" Asked a passerby.

Their neighbor on the east was papa Wagadugu who had a son called Rawlings- a blunt and frank no nonsense man. He governed his father's house so well until he passed it on to his younger brother. He told the gang, Master thief, his lapdog and her puppy dog to stop that hypocrisy because he saw that the gang and master thief were planning to kidnap Papa Elephant.

The Rumor Mill popular Newspaper said the other day that this time they may be in for a rude awakening because the grandkids of Papa Elephant are waiting for them. His kids are no more small and naïve like they were before.

What would you do in the place of Papa Elephant? What are the other kids of papa Africa doing? Why are they sitting quiet while Yankee, Marianne and Diana are kidnapping and raping their villages? Please leave Papa Elephant alone!

Until then, leave Papa Elephant alone!

# Chapter Four

# Ms. Haislmaier

## Vocabulary Preview

1. **Opprobrium**—Disgrace from shameful behavior.
2. **Coitus**—Sexual intercourse between male and female.

# Chapter Four

# Ms. Haislmaier

She was popularly known as Ms Haislmaier. She came from a rich and respectable family, but in that family, her household was the only poor one because her father chose to be a teacher and her mother a school mistress. However, they had what the other family members did not have. They grew up as a closely knitted family with her parents and siblings that if one of them was late or absent, the rest did not eat; they waited for the latecomer or absentee to come.

Ms Haislmaier was very very beautiful girl, but she did not believe it. Like most women today, she struggled with her self-esteem. She gave herself easily to men who did not love her just so she could win their love. She was taught in Sunday School that for her to fall in love with a man, he should show that he is ready to sacrifice his life for her, for that is the way the bible says a man should love his wife and be ready to die for her. If such commitment was not forthcoming, she should not get involve because love bought or begged cannot withstand trials and time.

No one can explain why she wanted to live like Mrs. Tannenholz or die like Mrs. Eggebraaten who got married to men they always tried to please and force to love them. The men cheated on them and finally dumped them at a time they needed them most. Mrs. Eggerbraaten's case was even worst because she had cancer when the husband dumped her. For Tannenholz, her husband felt she was too old for him; he ran around with younger women, so she too divorced him.

No one knows why she always wanted to live too like Ms. Igirigiachusim-a neighbor who always fell in love with crazy boys. Today Ms. Igirigiachusim drinks her past like gall as she regrets the insatiable gullibility with which she drank the fairytales on fairylands her men promised her.

For one reason or the other, Ms Haislmaier was always fascinated with bad and irresponsible boys because they were fun to her. If her brother wanted to irritate her, he sang her a song "why do beautiful girls like crazy boys". You smile; don't you? She always told him that she knew what she was doing. She had a child with a man who was more a sperm donor than a lover for immediately she got pregnant, the man ran away. Her family had to pick the pieces of her broken pots and raised her child to avert the **opprobrium** of the community.

Whether by curse or asininity, she always ran after men who did not love her. Her love experiments did not last long though **garnished** with **coitus.** In January 2001, a man carried her on his way to Pendleton as courtesy of his friend. She was going to see a man who did not love her. She told the driver that she had 2 boyfriends and was confused which one to keep. After she told him about their backgrounds and how they treated her, the driver told her to keep none.

The one she left in Lewiston had not called her despite knowing that she was traveling under bad weather. The driver intimated that it shows lack of concern and care from the men she was rolling in the hay with. The one she was going to see knew that she was coming, but he too had not called her since she traveled to Lewiston although he knew that she was traveling back to see him with bad weather. She always rationalized in defense of the men.

They decided to give them a test each. The driver asked her to call the first and tell him that she felt like she was pregnant and will be coming back to live with him. He told her that he was busy and will call her back. She waited but not even a fly buzzed, so she tried to call him again. All her attempts fell on his familiar voicemail. The driver called with his number and behold, he picked. So the driver was right to say men want sex, but they do not want the responsibilities that come with it. Do you want to know what happened with the second?

Needless to say that he gave her the wrong address to their house because he always wanted to meet her in that hotel or in her own house. The driver then used his wisdom to save her from being stranded. He told her to tell him that she has bought him some Christmas gifts and needed to give them to him. That is when he gave them the right address. Men nowadays always want to take from women; they want sex with no commitment.

In 2008, she fell in love again with a man she loved but who did not love her and spent his whole life cheating with other women. He flaunted cocottes before her, and she had heart attack and died days after. Whose fault was it that she could not find a loving and caring man who could make her his pearl?


Until then, may her soul find in heaven the love she missed on earth.

# Chapter Five

# Tales of Eat and Run

## Vocabulary Preview

1. **Commotion**—A condition of turbulence.
2. **Gushing**—To flow uncontrollably
3. **Populace**—public or inhabitants of a place.
4. **Pinhole**—A small hole made with a pin.
5. **Absconded**—To sneak away without people noticing you.

# Chapter Five

# Tales of Eat and Run

When I was in secondary school, an incident occurred with my mom. My mother was a petty trader who sold bushmeat pepper soup by the road side in Ancienne Gare Routière in Quartier Yabbasi-Douala. She was popularly known as Mami Anna.

There was a man who usually comes and eats and then runs away. When he arrived on that day, my sisters told me to place my eyes on him. I did. I asked him to pay before eating, but he said he would pay after eating. After he ate, he got up to go, and I told my mother. My mother told the other customers. He was detained by the other customers and passersby. Jungle justice at best!

A passerby heard about the **commotion**. He asked my mother what the man did. The people said "he eats from this widow and refuses to pay." So the passerby paid the money and asked the people to hand the man to him. Immediately as they handed the man to him, he began beating the man until blood was **gushing** out of his mouth, and nostrils. My mother had to go and give back the passerby's money, but he refused to take it. My mother threw the money on the floor saying, "for God's sake, it is not because of food that you will beat this man like this. Don't kill this man here and put us into trouble." The **populace** was telling my mother "go away woman, he has paid you. Let him deal with him the way he deems fit." If the police had not come, they would have killed that guy. So people should beware where they eat and run.

Another time was in 1991. I remember in Yaoundé seeing two young girls that we could call "ATM Drainers" or "Coffee Bang Feng" (coffee is ripe here) paraded naked in front of a restaurant because they ate and did not have money to pay. They came with a "Guyman" boyfriend who allowed them to pass their orders. One of them has been making the young man to spend and spend without letting him see the **pinhole.** He knew that the girl was merely using him up. Each time he invited her out to eat, she will bring her friends.

So he invited them to the restaurant where he allowed them to pass their orders as usual. They ate and drank like people who were leaving town. After some time, the man **absconded** and left abandoned them there at the restaurant. They were told to wash plates if they did not have money to pay, but they refused. The restaurant owner seized their clothes and sold them to a customer leaving them naked in front of the restaurant. After about two hours, the customer who bought the clothes came and gave them back their clothes. Then he asked them, "Vous allez venir encore manger ici sans payer? Voila leurs feses; espèce des bordelles". If it was today with electronic cameras, it would have been all over the net.

Until then, beware where you eat and run away.

# Chapter Six

# Natalie Munroe: Freedom Of Speech Muzzled By Absentee Parents.

## Vocabulary Preview

1. **Histrionics**—Emotional behavior
2. **Extolling**—To praise
3. **Muddle**—To make a mess or mix up.

# Chapter Six

# Natalie Munroe: Freedom Of Speech Muzzled By Absentee Parents

A teacherwas suspended with pay in February, 2011, for writing her personal blog about students. Are we still living in the country of the free and land of the brave? Sooner or later Americans are crossing oceans to go and teach others on freedom of speech. Teacher, teach thyself! American schools are in big trouble! Let me tell you guys some personal stories about our little angels. I tell you guys everyday that we are in an epoch called "childrenism" where children rule. Someday in future it will be "animalism" where your cat will be head of household or family head. The parentsI know you will make some noise after all, he that is crying and he that is laughing are all guilty of making noise. Now enjoy and make some noise!

One day a female teacher was leading her students to the cafeteria, and one of them asked to use the restroom. After entering, the student quickly bolted back out and asked the teacher "MS. (so and so), do you want to see me jack up." I was standing between the door of the cafeteria and the restroom door. Then the teacher exclaimed "no, he didn't." I asked her what happened, and she asked me what the young man said. I repeated it to her. I did not know what jack up meant. Being from Africa, I thought perhaps it was a form of exercise that he wanted to do, so I was wondering why she was angry. Methought it was just the habitual female **histrionics** where they always use a grenade to kill a cockroach. She explained to me that it means masturbation. I made a quick sign of the cross and said "Lord have mercy! These kids will come and rape someone here one day in broad day light." She reported the student to the administrators, and they asked her to write a report. I was shocked to hear that nothing happened to the student.

Another day a student wrote a wooden sign and placed it in front of her desk. The sign read "fuck me. Fuck my life y'all." Every time I taught and looked at her, she showed me the sign that read "fuck me". I will laugh, but the other students did not know why I kept laughing hard. She made me lose my thought each time I read that sign, so I asked her to step outside. She refused, and I called the administrators. One of them came, and she said that she did not have a sign. Immediately as she went back to class, she removed her sign that she had passed to her friends and placed it back in front of her. So I just said to myself, "don't be in a haste; you will have plenty of customers." I decided to ignore her and her sign and continued my job.

Another one always sang this song to me,

Nigger mother fucker, 3X

Nigger nigger mother fucker 2X

What you gonna do?

The administrators sent him to ISS for one day where he went and slept all day long. I actually liked the song because it was original. It meant at least he had one thing that he knew how to do-write music to say the least. I gave him a dollar for his creativity.

In one school, the principal said since kids do no more do homework, so the teachers should stop giving homework. Would that shock you that for seven years that school had never made the AYP, but surprisingly their principal was one time the state principal of the year? How? Isn't our society **extolling** mediocrity now?

So why are people crucifying the poor woman for nothing? America is shying away from the truth. The teacher did nothing wrong! If you look at things well; most parents who are angry about her admonishments are absentee parents who feel indicted for absentee parenting when the kids are called to responsibility. They are setting on time bombs. Just compare the education the kids receive today and what was yesteryears, and you will see that educational standards have been **muddled** up in excessive freedom. Isn't she covered too by the First Amendment?

Until then, give the woman's job back.

# Chapter Seven

# Sylvester: The Coffin Maker.

## Vocabulary Preview

1. **Stalling**—walk slowly.
2. **Wry**—dry or sardonic.

# Chapter Seven

# Sylvester: The Coffin Maker

When I visited home in 2001, I asked of one of my friends. My sister told me that he had become a coffin seller. I asked her to accompany me, so we could pay him a visit. I asked him about life and his business. He told us that all was well except for his business that was **stalling** because people have not been dying these days. Then he added a prayer request. He said he wanted God to blossom his business for him to have one of the biggest stores in the place. My sister tried to pull me away, but I resisted. And my sister just began going alone as if saying "ok if you want to be his customer, you should stay there alone because I am not. I am gone!"

Since I did not have much faith for the prayer topic, and we need faith for God to answer our prayers, I decided to send out an SOS. This was just because I am not too spiritual to honor his prayer request because I am afraid of it. Imagine that I was praying and God said ok Hamilton let us start with you as his first customer. So I am leaving it with you all to do the bombardment. I was seeking for prayer warriors to stand shoulder to shoulder with me and bombard heaven with intercession for my friend who makes coffins so that his business will prosper. Feel free to add fasting and speaking in tongues to expedite the request. Oh, if anyone is naming and claiming customers for him, they should spare me because I am my mother's first son. This may be the explained version of my request

My friend sells coffins or caskets, and he says he has been having bad business because people are no more dying for their families to buy his coffins. So he asked me for prayers so that people can die for him to have good business. Since I am not too spiritual to make such a prayer, and I have friends like you, I want you to help. The only condition I request is that please do not include me as one of his customers because I am the first son of my mother. Please always listen to the entire prayer topic before you pray, so you do not pray at the first request if not you will have to undo the prayer with 40 days and 40 nights of fasting and prayers.

Notwithstanding, no matter how awkward and **wry** his prayer request is, it is just a business. Most people want to be buried in coffins and imagine if he did no more sell coffins. Imagine if every coffin seller went out of business. Do you want the guy to die of bad business?

Until then, I am divided with wishing him good business and bad business.

# Chapter Eight

# Atungsiri and Atungkiri: One For Me, One For You.

## Vocabulary Preview

1. **Damnation.** Condemned to everlasting punishment.

# Chapter Eight

# Atungsiri and Atungkiri: One For Me, One For You

Three thieves had stolen things, and they felt that the best place to share their booty was in the graveyard since it was quiet and calm at night. When they reached there, they hid themselves in the bush, and one of them heard a voice. There were two people sharing things in the graveyard. His partner explained that "c'est le Diable et Dieu qui partagent les morts" (it is God and the Devil sharing the dead). They listened and listened attentively as the sharing continued. Un pour moi, un pour toi (One for me, one for you). One for me, one for you and one for me, one for you. It went on and on like that for about 15 minutes then one of the sharers said "je prend ceux deux ci, et tu prends les trois autres." It means; I take these two, and you take those other three. The guys in the bush thought that he was referring to them, so you make your guess. They ran helter-skelter. The question now is who do you think were sharing things in the graveyard? If it happened that you died today, and God and the devil were to share the dead, who do you think will own you? You cannot be unclaimed, for one of them must take you.

Many people are waiting for the end of the world, but the end of the world will come at anytime for everyone. If you die today, your world has come to an end, and you will only be waiting for the Judgment Day. If you do not die today, then you will wait till Jesus comes back and end this world. No matter when and how you die, your soul will be up for division. It must be owned by one person: either God or the Devil.

The Devil is known to own the souls of wicked people where he lives with them in hell and torment their souls day and night. There will be wailing and gnashing of the teeth. Your soul will no more die, and the fire is never quenched. It is called eternal **damnation.** If you are killing people or helping others to kill people, your soul will go to the Devil. If you are doing bad things, the Devil will pick your soul. If you are so selfish like the guy below, then the devil will own your soul.

On the other hand, God takes only godly people with him to heaven. So we may want to ask what godliness is then. Godliness is to obey God's word. Before Jesus left for heaven, he asked all of us to do two things: Love God with all our being and to love our neighbors as we love ourselves. So are we loving God or are we loving the things of the world? He that loves the things of the world makes himself /herself an enemy of God. If you become an enemy of God, God will not take your soul to heaven. There will be no more tears or sorrow; it is joy and joy everyday of eternity. There will not be any sickness there; no divorce, no death, and no politics. If you give your life to Christ first so that whatever good deeds you do he will sanctify them, your soul will go to God. If you see someone suffering and you help them, your soul will be picked by God. If you give food to those who are hungry, clothes to those who are naked, and health to those who are sick, God will pick your soul.

It is important to note that your good deeds alone will not give you salvation; you must confess with your mouth the Lord Jesus, and believe in your heart that God has raised him from the dead for you to be saved. Furthermore, simply because you are saved does not mean you should live any how; you will not also go to heaven.

On the last day when souls will be shared between the Satan and God, your soul will go to the devil because you did only the things that the devil wanted. If you did only the things that God wanted, your soul will go to God. So I ask you today;

who do you want to own your soul on the last day? You will only decide that with your lifestyle.

Until then, I want God to be the owner of my soul on the last day.

# Chapter Nine

# Paulina Turner: The Sad Life Of A Beauty

## Vocabulary Preview

1. **Happenstance**—coincidence, accident.
2. **Ephemeral**—temporal.

# Chapter Nine

# Paulina Turner: The Sad Life Of A Beauty

Paulina was born in Oregon and grew up in Oregon. She had never gone out of the country. When she was going to Washington, she told people she was going out of the country. Her parents were born in Oregon, they grew up in Oregon, and they died in Oregon. Her sister lived in one of the Washingtons-not quite sure whether the city or the state. On her beautiful face resided a constant and hospitable smile that was hard for a stranger to pass unwelcome. She spoke in an accent that was distinct of an Oregonian. Perhaps she was just flirty, but perhaps she was just kind and wanted the least of men to feel joyful talking to a beautiful girl like her. Hellas beneath that smile, she had issues every normal girl would have in addition to the ones that a beautiful girl of her caliber will have.

Actually she knew her boyfriend when she was 17, but she had had a lesbian tryst with a cousin who spent the night for a stay-over when she was 8. Despite all these boys she joked and flirted with, she feared she could grow fat or die alone. She was not promiscuous which made it difficult for her to really retain a man for long considering that most men nowadays shy away from the responsibility of marriage and just want **happenstance** and adventures.

The other women were jealous of her whether for her beauty or for her self confidence I don't know. Men envied her and made sexist statements if they could not get her friendship. The men that she had rejected slandered her that she was a lesbian. Those that have regarded her as a sex object were now discouraged and disappointed because no matter how much they tried, they could not sniff her panties. Finally, the neighborhood saw her with a guy she introduced as her boyfriend. He was a musician and the envy of all young girls in the neighborhood. Notwithstanding, she was still not fulfilled.

Why was she always sad within when she had the envy of most women: old and young? She had the beauty, she had the career, and she now has a companion. The truth about it is that she knew very well that the boyfriend did not have commitment as a principle and objective in life, but that was the type that made her look very fulfilled in front of her friends and enemies. She knew he was the type of boyfriend that if she lost a limb, he will dump her for the one with limbs, yet she consoled herself that the time had not come.

She was worried about getting fat which was like a chronic disease of most young girls, so she invested her time and resources in weight loss products and made the gym her living room. She was beautiful; yet with low self esteem. You knew it only when you were with her. She worried daily that she would one day end up alone, or if she had anyone, he was going to be an abuser or even a parasite that will suck blood and water from her until she sells herself to coping mechanism and then die finally at a young age. She was also too worried that men appreciated her sex appeal and beauty but not her intellect and her passion.

There were tail telling signs that she ignored. Although they were both into each other, they were not like minded. They wanted to have sex every minute of the day and wanted to be with each other every minute of their lives, but he was so money minded and did not consider family as important as she did. She has lived beauty and known that life was not all about beauty, but he was still striving to show people he was handsome. You have often heard that violence is the weapon of weak communicators. Her boyfriend had a pendulum temperament that swung by at home according to his day outside. They could never resolve their problems by themselves without him trying to involve his female friends. He will say "Angelica you are woman, is Paulina right? In addition, she wanted to further her education, but he thought education was a waste of time and money. Just the mere fact that he looked at her as a sex object could have opened her eyes, but she thought she will change him when they got married. She forgot that our people say "You can easily reform a boyfriend but not a husband; you tolerate the husband only." She knew that he had a lot of things she must change in him while he thought she needed to go to a survivor school to be street smart.

He had quickly noticed that there were many things she could do well but that was not what mattered to her boyfriend. He spoke to her in terms of a trophy he will hoist around but wanted to be replaced at anytime if it was not more the winning trophy. Her boyfriend has successfully kept his drug addiction and pornography away from her. Not sooner were they married did she start to see signs. Despite all the sex she gave him, he was still fantasizing about the girls outside. He flirted and was still on dating sites even though he was married. He kept female companions that they went out regularly to clubs and parks. As life may have it; she could remember the good men she turned down because of either color, height or wealth. Now she seems to have gotten stuck with the onetime Mr. Right who has become a match from hell. Paulina, who would you blame?

If you are a beautiful girl, know that beauty does not last forever. Garnish your beauty with virtues that are not **ephemeral**. Character does not hide; you should go for the man whose character will make your life joyful. And for those men who are married but want to live single lives, beware you will soon become single and looking. If you are married but want to live like you are single, you will never have a lengthy and happy marriage. Paulina, love and marriage are for people who want commitment so next time, go for the man who has shown great signs of commitment and care.

Until then, keep praying for Paulina.

# Chapter Ten

# Gabe Small

## Vocabulary Preview

1.  **Alluding—make reference**

# Chapter Ten

# Gabe Small

This article is in response to the young Ghanaian rapper from Tema called Gabe Small. Through this article, I want to encourage the young people especially the young boys who are rejected everyday by women they like. Are there flops in your menu that make you want to miss out some courses? Rosalind Russell once said "Flops are a part of life's menu and I've never been a girl to miss out on any of the courses." Many people go out to witness, but when their intended target rejects them, they get angry or stick around because they cannot fathom being rejected. Many men get rejected in life by women before they die. The men who are never rejected are those who never actually speak or spoke to women. If they did, one or two will reject them.

Women are seldom rejected, but each time they have been rejected, there was nothing like their fury. Two classic examples are Lady Potiphar who was rejected by Joseph, and Tamar who was rejected by Judah. Nonetheless, everyone is rejected at some point in life, but the difference is at the level of reception and reaction. How should you react when rejected by a love interest.

For some, I will say smack the dust off you feet and go you way, for they do not even merit your love. If a woman wants you, she will give you no reason. If you live in a hole, she will follow you into that hole and if you live in the sky, she will fly with you. But if she does not want you, she will give you 101 reasons and will tell you how you speak like Mickey

Mouse. For others, give a little bit of patience knowing that it takes some people time to make up their minds.

However, if someone does not show you interest, leave them alone. Don't kill yourself because someone rejected you, for you have only one life; meanwhile, you can find their replacement in life. Everyone in life will be rejected at some point in time. Not everyone is married to the person they truly love and though they did not marry the person they truly loved, they are still very happy. Stay patient because some day their replacement will come. If you die, you will never live to see their replacement and prove to them that they made a bad choice. You need to stay alive to show them that despite them, you are happy and perhaps they are not. I say stay alive and not die.

Writers are aware of how publishers rejected them. E.E Cummings' manuscript was rejected 15 times before it was published by his mother. If I close this exordium without **alluding** to the master of rejection: Jesus Christ, then I have failed in my purpose. The prophet Isaiah in chapter 53:3 wrote "He is despised and rejected of men; a man of sorrows, and acquainted with grief: and we hid as it were our faces from him; he was despised, and we esteemed him not."

Therefore, stay alive for in life in general, it is not everyone who will like you or accept you. It is not everyone who will believe in you, and it is not everyone who will follow you in what you do. Why keep any love that is like a dove in the cage when it is future heartbreak? No matter what you do to it, it will fly away if you open the cage. True love should be like the flesh of your flesh and bone of you bones; it is going nowhere, no matter how much flesh and how many other ribs are out there. Once more, I encourage you to rise above your rejection and stay alive. If you are running after the person you love for five miles and he/she does not seem to wait for you, give up, for you may be chasing the wind. Do not run after a woman as if she does not see you because if she wanted you, she will run after you too even if you were in a hole. Ask God for the key of life, and you will live in abundant life.

Until then, may God bring your true love.

# Chapter Eleven

# Kadidiatou

## Vocabulary Preview

1. **Maquillage--** makeup
2. **Flaneur**—a loafer, idler.

# Chapter Eleven

# Kadidiatou

My name is Kadidiatou. I am the lady who just passed here with the veil. When I am with my husband I wear the veil but when alone I do not. That immediately reminded me of Nathaniel Hawthorne's The Minister's Black Veil. Perhaps it is true every human being is wearing a veil. Don't you think you might be wearing a veil?

It is now customary to behave differently in public from the way we behave in secret. That is why during the day and in church the pastor preaches on holiness and at night he is driving to pick up a 13 year old girl for sex. Perhaps every human has a veil. That is why you speak differently when no one is around and when someone is around your speech is polished. You use all sorts of expletives when on your own and you know that the acquiescent majority will not condemn you but when you face a fastidious majority you sound like Angel Michael. Don't you think you might be wearing a veil?

In public you call your wife: honey, sweetie, bon bon but when only the two of you, you call her bitch, prostitute, loser. You know that you do not treat your wife well at home but you want everyone to think you are the best husband. In public you say I love my wife and in private you say if not of your mother I would not have married you. People look at you walk in public and envy you as a happy couple but back in your home each of you sleeps in a different rooms and when you sleep on the same bed your backs face each other. Yes, you are fighting and a knock is on your door, you quickly put some **maquillage** and show up at the door with a smiling face. Don't you think you might be wearing a veil?

Can anyone reconcile who you are behind the keyboard and what you are in person? Well there are screen names now that people use to veil themselves. Are you the same person scamming people through the computer? Are you the same person living as a call girl from the comfort of your home but everybody knows you are a student. As you know no one wears a mask forever. That mask will always fall off. So too does no one wear a veil forever.

Let me ask you this: is there a time that if someone kept your person in public you will be different from the one in secret; straight in the morning and gay at night. To the community you are married but on the internet you are single and looking. Yes, the veil of a loving husband to the neighbors but behind the veil lies an adulterer, murderer, **flaneur,** embezzler; planting evil in innocent lives. You know that your veil will soon fall off and people will know the real you.

You offer gifts to strangers worldwide, but your own family and those who live in the same house with you never know when you have money. At home poverty is killing you, but outside every passerby takes a beer on your budget.

Do you know anyone who is wearing a veil? I mean not you; someone else. Would you tell me why that someone is wearing a veil? This world was made bare and its inhabitants must live bare so that what they are without is the person within. It is better for people to think you are bad and when they come closer, they realize you are wonderful, than for them to think you are mother Teresa, but when they come, they realize you are Erzebet Bathory.

Until then, those who wear veils end up as strangers to themselves.

# Chapter Twelve

# Dr. Empty Mop

*At the hospital*

**Doctor:** hello Kpanfiri, how are you. My name is Empty Mop. I will be your doctor as from today.

**Kpanfiri:** thank you doctor. You look a nice person. I really like the way you are confident. Do you think I gonna get well?

**Doctor:** Sure, looking at you, you can make it. You will get well soon. Just stay put; do not move. Open your eyes, take off your shirt. Turn your back. You have a scar behind your back. When did that happen?

**Kpanfiri:** Oh well when I was a little kid, I was playing with my sister and she mistakenly stabbed me on my back.

**Doctor:** was your sister a demon? Is she still mean to you? By the way how did you react?

**Kpanfiri:** Yeah yeah yeah, she was when we were kids though. But now she is married. When she was getting married I was sorry for the boyfriend. I told him he was going to die before his time.

**Doctor:** Is he dead yet?

**Kpanfiri:** Well you asked me before how I reacted. Well I just cried and left it like that. Oh my brother in-law is still alive and they are happily married. Surprise, Surprise!

**Doctor:** Yes, you did the right thing. Well stand on this machine. Well let us do this first. Take this cup, go to the restroom, piss inside this cup and then shit and bring some to me.

*Kpanfiri leaves and comes back with two cups all of them filled to the brim.*

**Doctor:** go drop it on that window.

**Kpanfiri:** Thank you.

**Doctor:** Ok now take off your short. Lean on this machine, stop breathing and look straight. Do you see that woman there in front of you? Just look at her eyes. Great, Sit over there and wait for me I will be back.

*Kpanfiri goes to the waiting room. Two hours later a nurse calls him back into the doctor's room*

**Kpanfiri:** Hey doctor, good news?

**Doctor:** Mr. Kpanfiri, your case is bad. Your lungs are rotten because of smoking. Too much alcohol is ruining your bronchioles and nerves. Even your liver has been affected. There is a nerve behind your back that is dead. You also have serious hemorrhoids.

**Kpanfiri:** yes, I like to eat garri and meat only. How bad is that?

**Doctor:** don't you see that your anus is almost falling out. Anyway, it was nice knowing you and being your doctor. Go home and rest in peace.

**Kpanfiri:** doctor, no medicine no prescription?

**Doctor:** I do not prescribe anything to anybody. I am only specialized in diagnostics.

**Kpanfiri:** what type of quack doctor are you? If you knew you do not prescribe why tell me all these sicknesses. Now you have made me to be afraid. I will have to talk to the board. Where did you get your license? Always diagnostics but no solutions!

**Doctor:** go get loss mbut man. Did you see a signboard that Kpanfiri come to Doctor Adiburoja for consultation? I just told you my specialty is diagnostics and you are hitting your head on the wall. Go get loss elsewhere. Na me I give you sickness look at my problems. Next

A new patient is ushered in as Kpanfiri is booted out.

*Lesson: This play is reminiscent of the many people who always make proper diagnostics but never prescribing anything; they raise the problem but do not propose solutions. That is the zenith of hopelessness.*

# Chapter Thirteen

# The Wind and The Iroko

## Vocabulary Preview

1. **Sardonic--** mocking
2. **Heralded--**publicized

# Chapter: Thirteen

# The Wind and The Iroko

When I say "Arabian nights" you will answer "Entertainment". Arabian Nights? Good! Old men and women, I have a story to tell you. My story is about the wind and the iroko tree.

Once upon a time, there was a man who thought he was the king. He gathered his entire village, and they went to witness the wind demonstrate its strength in the forest. He walked, and walked, thinking the entire village was behind him. When he reached the forest, he realized that no one was behind him, and that he had just taken a walk to the forest. There he remembered that, if a man thinks he is leading, but he has no one following him behind is merely taking a walk. Nonetheless, the king rather than go back, decided to enjoy the show.

Long time ago, the wind thought it was the strongest. It was involved in a battle with the grass. So when it passed, it pushed all the grass down, and the grass slept sideways. The wind drummed its chest all over and invited all the animals and kings to come and witness its strength. "At last I am the king of the land, and I will show you all". The wind said.

So the animals and kings gathered to watch the wind demonstrate its strength. It passed and blew again this time stronger than before. The grass slept sideways, and the little trees fell off their roots. "It is now the new beginning" the wind whispered. The forest will be different because there was a new king for the entire land it publicized. To the wind and its friends, it was the long sought victory they had longed for.

Suddenly the **sardonic** laughter of the Tortoise **heralded.** As everyone looked, it said: "listen, why do you push the grass and you are happy thinking you have won the battle. You have not; actually you make more noise than anything. The Iroko has not budged since you have been blowing. It has always been in the same place. Immediately, the wind realized that just because it screams aloud victory, it does not mean it has won.

No matter how many times or how much a boxer claims it has won a match, if his or her hand has not been lifted up by the referee, then it has not won; it is only making noise. Let the wind blow harder or shout louder that it is setting order in the forest; every other animal in the bush knows it is only making noise because the wind has failed to remove the Iroko.

Until then, it is noise making for the wind to claim victory in the forest.

# Chapter Fourteen

# Marylyn

## Vocabulary Preview

1. **Meted** – To distribute by measurement.
2. **Vent** – To express one's feelings.
3. **Cumbersome**—Awkward and heavy to carry.
4. **Ambrosia**—Food of the gods.
5. **Penury**—Great poverty.

# Chapter Fourteen

# **Marylyn**

She told everyone that she was 29, but her real age was 19. She only told you if you showed compassion and care. She did it with a smile of vengeance. When she introduced her name, she annotated that it is like Marylyn Monroe. She has to tell a lie to those who ask her age just to make the men who approached her justified. Justified not for the right punishment they **meted** on her but for using her as a toilet tissue. She did not tell anyone what she did for a living, but she wanted to know what you did for a living. Once she knew what you did for a living, then she asked your purpose of talking to her. She had a lot in her stomach to **vent** out, and no one was going to deny her the golden opportunity. So listen to her chronicle.

Marylyn is from Hungary the same country that Kellie Pickler had never heard of. She was lured into Austria first to work in a restaurant, but it soon turned to something else. There was no work, and she needed money to save her mother and family from some cumbersome debts that had seized joy away from her. How could she look at her mother into the face and eyes while she cries and struggles to make ends meet? She thought to herself that between her legs lie **ambrosia** that even gods have not been able to bypass the temptation and what more of mere mortal men who lose their souls by just seeing a skirt in the dark.

She smiled and giggled as dimples widen on her jaws. If there is anything as a beautiful woman, she was the epitome thereof. Her face was like a painted or retouched picture of a Victoria Secret model, and her body was smooth and silky that it glittered like a golden dining table on which the rich satisfied the desires of their flesh. Every man will like to lick from her table.

Immediately you spoke to her, and she trusted you, she told you that she was a prostitute, and she f....s men for money. If you showed any compassion, she discouraged you from having that pity party. "You should not, for I began it two months ago when I realized that men always dumped my mother and left her with a sad heart and no money to pay her bills." She will justify her act. Due to **penury**, she dropped out of school and felt that she could make it. She was like a chemical reaction in which lebensfreude had been emptied out and replaced with schadenfreude. She became very happy to see men suffer because her father left her and her mother while she was 8, and every man she has met only wanted to go through her legs. Worst still, they were never reliable! They promised to stay in touch and help, but when they left, you never heard from them again.

She did not believe men make promises because those who ventured into making one or more never kept one or all. She thought that everyman who saw her only had one assignment that Satan had given him: have sex with her. Most of the men who have had sex with her were twice or thrice older than her; they were mostly drunk, and also married too. "I see their married rings, and I will say to them 'you are fu..ing me here and your poor wife is at home'." She confessed. One of them got mad and slapped her after she said that. Some men come very spiritual, but she **entices** them by showing her nakedness. "Once I show them what they want, they forget their spiritual vows". She boasted.

To Marylyn, there is only one thing that goes through the mind of a man when he sees a woman: sex. Do you agree with her? She thinks every man wants to have sex with her, and they do not really care about her as a person. Do men really care? Now she has sex with them for revenge and not for love. Would you do that? She sees sex as a means of retaliating on men for their exploitation and evil ways. Marylyn told everyone that she uses sex to empty their pockets and then leave them miserable. Can women do that? Gentlemen, if you are misusing a lady out there, know that you are hurting even her daughters or neighbors' daughters who are watching. Please, treat women right for they are weaker vessels!

Until then, I wish her well.

# Chapter Fifteen

# Riflo Rifala

## Vocabulary Preview

1. **Denizen**—citizen.
2. **Schadenfreude**—happiness to see people suffer.
3. **Lugubriously**—dismal, sorrowful.
4. **Paripassu**-- Side by side.
5. **Rictus**—a cry with the mouth wide open.

# Chapter Fifteen

# **Riflo Rifala**

Riflo as he was popularly known was born in Nnewi. His father was from Nnewi and his mother was from Onitsha, so he was between Nnewi and Onitsha but a **denizen** of neither. Between these two cities were business savvy geniuses who could sell a hen in a bag or even sell you the egg as a hen. When he is on the phone, you will think he is quarreling with someone, but you will only know he is enjoying when he starts to laugh like thunder. For one reason or the other, that spirit of business did not seem to flow in his vein because no matter what he tried to do, he failed in it woefully. He had had so many failures that, as if fueled by **schadenfreude**, some people sarcastically and sardonically called him Riff Raff. A business idea came to his mind; that of starting a church. Him and another companion in misery decided to do a joint venture. Then one day, I say one day, their star shone.

Riflo and his friend met a juju man who told them that he had a potion that could attract even the most hardened of criminals to follow him. Riflo explained to his friend that they did not have anything to lose in trying it. They contributed some money and made a down payment for their juju. It was given to them in a small bag that they needed to keep **lugubriously** underneath the pulpit on their altar. When the bag is placed there, anyone passing had to stop to attend service there and give them offerings before they continued to their own church or go home if they were no more going to church. Their church was growing, and they were now the talk of the town as two mighty men of God demonstrating the power of our Lord Jesus Christ with signs and wonders.

From mouth to ear, radio to villages and TV to cities, their news went across the place about the covenant Church of Our Lord. Whether to seek Jesus or to show off people came to their church. Underneath that physical growth laid a serious schism between Riflo and his friend. His friend felt marginalized because Riflo was not sharing their spoils or booty *pari passu.* He had tried for Riflo to consider that they were partners and not master and subordinate to no avail. As you know, the love of money is the root of all evil. Consequently, at the time that Riflo and his friend were gaining some gravitas, calamity struck. Armed robbers broke into Riflo's house and stole only that bag.

When the robbers left, Riflo began to cry. He sobbed and cried, mourned and wept until mucus mixed with tears dripped from his nostrils and eyes to form a homogeneous compound like baby lotion. When they asked Riflo what the robbers took, he merely uttered a **rictus** and cried louder. Church members tried to console him, promising to make donations so that he will replace what the canker worm had eaten. The more they promised and tried to console him, the more he cried. Finally, he told the people that it was his evangelism bag.

So the church members and volunteers each promised to donate a hundred fold so that the content of the evangelistic bag will be replaced. They imagined that in an evangelistic bag would only be a bible and some tracts. To Riflo, it was more than that. He cried again because he knew that in a few days the source of his membership growth will be severed. That made him weep the more. A few days later, his coworker announced he will be leaving him to start his own church. There, riflo began nursing a feeling of suspicion, but he did not know how to say it. That same church that was bubbling a few weeks ago is now going dry like a creek in the dry season. You see water in the morning and but in the evening, there is no more any water. Riflo cried again, this time asking neighbors and well-wishers if they had seen his evangelistic bag.

When Riflo's coworker began his own church, he dug the pulpit and buried the bag with its juju content in it. The same exponential growth they had experienced with Riflo was now his portion. Riflo now was convinced his friend had played the trick on him. He fulminated and cautioned to spill the bean if he did not surrender the bag. He contacted his friend's uncle and told him to warn his nephew to bring his evangelistic bag. His friend told his uncle that it is not an evangelist bag; that Riflo Rifala had something he was hiding and that he should come out clean. He bedaubed him to no effect.

Riflo's church had finally gone dead. He waited until his friend was coming out of church and he attacked him. The parishioners separated them and some elders took them into a room for brotherly negotiations. There, in there, his friend will reveal that the said bag Riflo Rifala has been mourning for is no evangelistic bag as he put it; it is a juju bag they used to win members into their church. The members dug out the bag, burnt it. At the time they were burning it, Riflo and his friend both cried and were holding each other as true companions they were in their previous time of distress. Together in unison, they cried the juju bag and again the mucus from their nostrils and tears from their eyes formed a homogenous mixture, this time like baby vomit. The devil gave, the devil has taken. When the devil gives you anything, he associates it will evil. That was the last time I ever heard or saw Riflo Rifala. I don't know if he has died by now or he has started another church. Do you know where he lives?

Until then, Riflo Should count on the power of God to work for Him.

# Chapter Sixteen

# Regina Boyderfield

## Vocabulary Preview

1. **Rampant**—uncontrolled, unbridled, unchecked.

# Chapter Sixteen

# **Regina Boyderfield**

I did not understand why Christians could not find mates in their respective churches until I met Regina. Regina Boyderfield attended a very big church with a male who played in their church band. Regina liked Lucas, but he was not aware. The brother did not seem to have a self-worth or good self-esteem. Regina told her friend that she had seen a young man in church she liked, but he did not seem to have her time. The friend advised her to go closer to catch his attention. She did to no avail. Surprisingly, on May 24, 2004, she was surfing the net and fell on the profile of Lucas where he has written "single and looking". He was very opened but did not have a fixed target yet. Regina approached him, and they began talking. They exchanged numbers and were talking. They finally made arrangements to meet. Then one day Lucas seeing the picture of Regina said "I seem to know this face." "Yeah, maybe," she replied, "Do you live in Kansas City? Do you attend this church?" To all the questions, Regina answered yes. Lucas was broken. He did not know someone from the church has finally met him looking for a mate out of a church of thousands of people.

She always told the men who met her in person that she had a boyfriend just to wade them off, but year after year she was single. She did not consider keeping a promise as important because she will tell you she was coming but will never show up. She did not know that those things counted towards her and nature paid her back with men who did not love her. I mean men too who could not keep promises. That is the hypocrisy that is **rampant** all over the churches. Regina weeded the keys of her keyboard for a mate, yet tended a blind eye to the people in her churches. If a brother said, "can I talk to you a minute," she will measure his height with her eyes from his toes to hair. Then slowly, she will walk away. At times she will say "nope!" In economics, business is good and prosperous when it is near to raw materials. Why does especially Regina pretend she doesn't like a man but will talk with the same man behind the veil of the net? Why do we always want to get involved with the unknown?

Regina did not know life is too short to be knocking the wrong doors and asking for love from the wrong people. She did not also know that internet love is easy for players but dangerous for serious people because very few people really succeeded. She will have to double her steps of faith should double. The stakes and the risks are too high. Yeah, real high!

She has been bypassing many men in her churches toiling on the net. Another mind told her that the people who should look for love from the internet are those with no churches or whose membership is too small because their chances of finding a partner in that church are limited. Because personal contact is very difficult in the developed world, the internet could be the easiest of planes to take them to that destination of love. But Regina has always come from a church with at least 300 members. There should be someone there for her. Instead, she and her friends who come from mega churches or churches of thousands like those of Eddie Long, Creflo Dollar, Del Brown, T.D Jakes, John Hagee, Marilyn Hickis, Joyce Myers and a lot more invade the internet looking for partners. Are churches failing Regina and her friends or Are Regina and her friends failing themselves? I am merely a narrator, so I don't have an answer.

Regina even thought about going back to her hometown to get married. Perhaps she should rather build her self-confidence or accept their spiritual family overseas or even both. Why can't the foreign men be her husband when they are fit to be her brothers in Christ? Are there no men in those churches whom she could marry here in America? She lacks self-confidence, and secondly, she does not want to "corrupt herself with foreign men". Consequently, she travels to space looking for love when love is on earth. Regina, look around you and select a spouse. There is no perfect man on earth! There is no Mr. Right or Soulmate. These people are already sitting in heaven. The ones here are broken pots that have and could be repaired by the master Porter called Jesus Christ.

Until then, stop looking for Mr. Right in the wrong places.

# Chapter Seventeen

# Judith Bushfaller

## Vocabulary Preview

1. **Embittered**—poisoned, bitter, angry.

# Chapter Seventeen

# **Judith Bushfaller**

"You see that Judith like that, we grew up in the same house. We ate in the same plate. Her mother and my mother were best friends." A pale voice in a slender body echoed. "Boy, let me tell you if you don't know. When we were little, we used to go to the farm together." He continued. It would seem he had a lot in his stomach that he wanted to throw out. After all; don't our people say that the porcupine has hidden things in its stomach until its entrails have been **embittered**? His friend too, a man with similar stature listened as if the priest was ready to make an ablution. Time and again he will interject intermittently a question or a provocative comment. "Obab is that how you were with that girl?" "Do you know the stream that is just behind that coconut bush?" Obab boastfully asked. "We used to go and swim there." He pointed to a river on his left. "Sometimes we did mami and papa too." Obab narrated to assert himself. "Massa, you too be don worry oh (boy, you have been the man)?" His friend praised him. "Na small one (is it small). I be di shake shake shake (I have animated the place)." He uttered his braggadocios. "But, na nyango that since wey i don go Etas, i don forget me (But that is the lady, since she went to the United states, she has forgotten me)." Obab lamented. "Boy, you di learn nga dem da so (man, you are only learning women)." His friend amplified the evil nature of women.

Judith went to the US with a Green Card, and she was braiding hair in one salon. Judith did not have a trade, and she did not have a career. How were they expecting her to start sending them money is only God alone who knows. More so, Judith was only one, they who are left at home are many. They can each remember her, but she cannot remember all of them. They should be the ones to contact her and say "Judith please don't forget me. Instead, they assume that Judith should remember all her friends, relatives and neighbors. Even if she remembered everybody, she could not call everybody. So Judith had to stay in touch with those who stayed in touch and forget those who did not. The pressures of moving to a new place, and the pressures of the family and friends expecting money from her became cumbersome. Judith lived abroad, but her physiognomy was like that of a grandmother in the village.

Then on Tuesday, January 12, 2009 one of her friends called her. " Allo, allo, allo allo, and Judith answered, " yes, allo, yes, allo." "Na Obab, na Obab" (It is me Obab, it is me Obab). He seemed to be repeating everything as if Judith going overseas is now deaf. "My mami eh Obab, you still dey alive so?" (Oh gosh, Obab, you are still alive). Judith exclaimed. "Why shouldn't I? You cannot just go there and forget your own people like that. Even if I was too small like an ant, you should not have forgotten me." Obab expressed his anger." "Weh Obab, nice to hear from you again. I am happy for you." She added. "Judith, you would have heard that I was dead already. I mean since you went to America then everything began falling apart for me. You know my mother passed away. My uncle's brother who was like his father also died. Oh, did you know that my other sister who was always insulting you like that, she too just died. Then now my mom just passed away." " weh Obaba, you have too much badluck. Weh obab, ashia. I am so sorry." Judith consoled him. "Judith, that is why I called you. What are we going to do again? Now is not the time to cry; it is a time to mourn. Please, I am the first boy, and I want to make the death celebrations for all these people before you hear that I am mad. If I did not remember that I had a friend like you in America, I should have killed myself." Obab told Judith.

"So Judith are you married now?" He asked trying to find out if he could sweettalk Judith into thinking he was interested in her. "I am also still single." Judith remembered their childhood, adolescent, and teenage days. She thought how Obab used to provide for her and defend her. She has had some men in between but none was like Obab. She said, "Obab, I will send you some money tomorrow." "Judi, Judi , that is my girl. Hahahahaha" he laughed a loud. "Judith, I knew that you will never forget me." Obab sang her flummery. To Judith, one good turn deserves another. It was not that she had forgotten her cronies and relatives; it was just that she could not think of all of them. They needed to reposition themselves into her mind because the worries of the foreign land shortened her memory.

Until then, if someone you know traveled, you should call or write them to stay in touch.

# Chapter Eighteen

# Ta Joe & Edimoley

Behind Pharmacie Du Rail lived two friends. Ta Joe was from Dschang while Edimoley was from Ebolowa. They were both in between 5.1 and 5.3 in height. They had lived in Douala for more than 20 years that they spoke more Pidgin than French and English. Except you knew them personally, you will always think that they were Anglophones. Both were very smart gentlemen when alcohol was away from them. If they ventured out together, they must fight. They were very very mischievous whether under the influence of alcohol or sobriety. I had visited Edimoley in his rewinding workshop where he repaired fridges, irons, compressors and other hydraulic motors. One Bafoussam woman came to him to repair the motor of her grinding machine. Edimoley asked her to give him money so he could buy her the parts, but she refused because she did not trust technicians. As a result, she went to buy it herself. Behind, Edimoley told me that he was still going to cheat her. He told me that these Bamileke women always think that they are smart. He advised me to watch how he was going to escheat her of her new part.

The woman quickly came back with smiles, happy that she just bought a new part. Edimoley smiled with the corners of his mouth foreshadowing mischief. He took the tiny part up, and the woman looked up. He brought it down, and the woman looked down. He took it up again, and the woman's eyes followed. He brought it down, and she too looked down. At that point, he began to repeat the process until the women's eyes got wearied that she could no more repeat the up and down movement. He quickly exchanged it with the old one that was by the side. After all, the old one was not even bad; the machine needed just some washers. He will later sell the new part to the next customer.

Ta Joe on the other hand was a builder. He built embankment walls. Unlike Edimoley, Ta Joe did his job very well and with honesty. He was happy to work and happier when the customer was satisfied. However, his lack of proper education always landed him into trouble even when Edimoley was the cause.

On July 21, 1988, Ta Joe and Edimoley went to a sack cloth removal ceremony. Both were drunk as was their habit of getting drunk in every party they attended. Edimoley started a fight and bottles were flying from one end to the other, tables landing on surfaces and women and even some men screaming for their dear lives as they rushed out for cover. There were 4 guys on Edimoley, so Ta Joe fearing for his life, went to Commissariat 6eme (just opposite Hotel Arista) to report the matter and bring the police.

Ta Joe liked to speak English, but I doubt if English liked for him to speak it. He said, "I have my friend in dangjey (as they pronounced danger in French). When he drinks, he behaves, but when I drink, I don't behave." Behave to have meant misbehave while don't behave means behaving well. They asked him why he was not behaving. They kept beating him and asking him if he was not going to behave again. Ta Joe will scream, "I nodi behave, na Edimoley di always behave sah." The police officer asked him once more "why you no di behave". Ta Joe said "because I di respect myself sah. Na my friend nodi behave sah". The police officers misunderstood him and instead took him for the trouble maker. They beat the more and locked him up.

Then the police officers went to the fight area, and eyewitnesses said they have sent someone who knows how the fight began to come and call for the police, but he has not come back. They told them that the trouble maker has gone home. One of the police officer's realizing they were holding the wrong guy said, "Il parait –il qu'on a enfermé la mauvaise personne (it seems we have the wrong person)." So they hurriedly went and released Ta Joe.

When Ta Joe came home the next day, we asked him why he was locked up. He narrated that he told the officers that "when me I drink, I nodi behave, but when Edimoley drink I di behave." We all understood the police officers did not know that behave was a parlance which meant misbehavior. For example, it was common for someone who was angry to ask you, "Do you want me to behave here?" What they actually meant was, "do you want me to misbehave here?" Students at times always said "I no behave for that test" which meant they did not do well. So locking Ta Joe up was a miscarriage of justice and lack of touch police officers because he was actually the better person of the two.

Until then, do not behave when you drink, for it may land you in jail.

# Chapter Nineteen

# **Perptua**

When Perptua was going to Bamenda, it was brother Sama who trekked with her for perhaps 2:45 mins. When she had problems with her registration, it was brother Sama who went with her to Yaoundé. He went to her class every morning to tell her good morning. When Perpe was sick, it was Sama who slept with her in the hospital for two weeks. He was so into Perpe that gainsayers called him woman wrapper. Unbelievers said he was the nadir of the aphorism "monkey di work baboon di chop." I had advised Sama not to give up, so his persistence made others to think that Perpe had bewitched him. I used to say, "Sama, good things do not come easily especially because women and pendulums are synonyms. .She may swing one day to you. One day, one day, Perpe will knock at your door" I will add impetus!

Unfortunately, when a Bambui guy who worked and lived in Bamenda came to town, his uncle took him to church. He fell for Perpe and swept her off her feet. He was tall, athletic, economically buoyant and the talk of both the town and village. All qualities Perpe fantasized about in her subconscious and conscious nature. They got married in late 1991. Sadly, I had graduated and left Bambui.

In 1992, I was on my way to Bambui to visit the brethren I left there. I stopped at Sister Sally's house in Bamenda. As I was eating the rice and drinking the Top Anana she served, she asked me, "Brother Arrey," as we were accustomed to calling each other, "did you know sister Perpetua?" I said "yes, who doesn't know Perpe." "She is in the hospital and we don't know if she will even get well. We have been praying for her but now that you have come, please let us go, so you will pray for her." Sally informed me. I quickly stopped a taxi, and we went there. At the hospital, the nurses refused that we should see her except her relatives. I told them that I was her pastor and have come to pray for her. We went in, and once she saw us, she smiled and called, "brother Arrey, Sister Sally" in such a faint voice. She had bruises all over her face, her hand and head were bandaged liked Lazarus from the grave, and her feet were suspended as if she had a car accident where she was the only survivor.

I asked Perpe what happened. She said one word, "Andrew" and began crying. Sally said, "Brother Andrew na yi massa." I felt so bad as she sobbed the more fighting these words through her tears, "Brother Arrey, I should have listened to you. Before you entered, you came to my spirit, and I remembered how you used to say 'marry the person who loves you most and not the one you love most. The one who loves you most will feel like they do not merit you and will treat you like their only world'." I smiled and little pride entered into me that one of my prophecies was fulfilled. That is how much we were close as brethren that our spirits communicated together. Then she continued, "This morning, my younger sister told me that she went to our house to take some of my clothes, and Andrew had a girl there. His girlfriend said my sister must knock before entering the house. " For more than a month that I am here, Andrew has been here only once; I mean, one time brother Arrey."

I muttered that those were grounds for divorce; abandonment and infidelity. Sister Sally quickly interrupted me that "the bible is against divorce." I smiled and asked Perpe if she was in contact with Sama. She said she did not know his whereabouts, but Sally interjected that she had met him sometime at Mbengwi Market. I said "we could go there right now.' So we went there, and Sama had his small secretariat he did documents. He was too elated to see us. I told him that Perpe was barely hanging on her life. He shuddered as if a part of him was in trouble. "Which hospital is she?" He asked. I told him. He quickly closed his store, and we left for the hospital. When we saw Perpe and she saw Sama, she almost jumped from her bed to embrace him, but the nurse stopped her, "Perpe it is not time for you to start standing." She was just too happy to see Sama again. Thenceforth, Sama took over the visitation and even part of the hospital bill. Miraculously and graciously, the Lord healed her that she even became more beautiful.

In 2001, when I went home, they had already been married for eight years, and they are still happily married today. They had written me a letter telling me how grateful they were for the role I played in creating their terrestrial felicity. They said, "Brother Arrey, marriage is sweet. We don't know why some people are not happy in their own marriages." Sama's shortcomings that Perpe saw have been conquered by his love, acceptance and value for her that they lived a happy life because Perpe married the person who loved her most and not the one she loved best.

It is divine and natural for men to run after women and not the other way round. Perpe finally had someone who adored her because he felt he did not merit her. Therefore, if a woman sees herself running after a man, she should consult the oracles because something is grievously wrong with her. Can you remember someone who was ready to die for you? Go and call them or go to the net and write them now. Don't let their shortcomings purloin your earthly bliss! That will be shortsighted!

Until then, insist more on people's strengths than their shortcomings.

# Chapter Seventeen

## Akiaekeme

### Vocabulary Preview

1. **Spinster**—an unmarried woman
2. **Buttressed**—to reinforce, to add impetus.
3. **Lebensfreude.** Joy of living.

# Chapter Twenty
# Akiaekeme

As I was driving last month, I remembered Akiaekeme, a divorced **spinster** who even had fewer men talking to her about marriage. She had news about everyone's marriage, everyone's child, everyone's husband, everyone's job and everyone's life. She knew whose husband was beating who, who was sleeping with who or whose child had dropped out of school. Perhaps she was not happy that others were not divorced like her or were going to get married and graduate from the Princesses of Our Fathers (a spinsters' club) she promoted with every pint of her blood. When she got a victim, she took her to the gossip laboratory and by the time the victim came out, hell would be a comfort zone or a familiar territory.

I don't know if it was a Thursday or a Friday, but I know that it was towards the end of the week that Adesuwa (Benin; meaning the crown of beauty) visited her, and she told her that her Husband was sleeping with her cousin. "Did I not say it" Akiaekeme exclaimed. "These men are never serious" she **buttressed** her point with her Ido accent because both of them were from Benin although they lived in Douala.

It is unknown if Adesuwa was aware of the Iago syndrome in Shakespeare Othello. If you have not read it, please do so because some of your problems may be ensuing from the ignorance thereof. The Iago syndrome is a desire to heap schadenfreude on the person whom you think has escheated you from your **lebensfreude.** It is also the spirit of excessive obsession with the sex lives of others. Akiaekeme did not want Adesuwa (her best friend or so it seemed) or any other young girl in the quarter to marry. As a result, she fabricated stories to destroy their relationships with the pretext that she was protecting them from hurt. She pretended to build a fence around them to prevent sorrow from coming in, but she left a chink through which she surreptitiously smuggled sorrow in. Adesuwa failed to see her covert war although she was aware of her fiends' overt wars.

Othello like Adesuwa was not aware of the Iago syndrome, so he thought that Iago was protecting him. Unfortunately, it was Iago who poisoned his mind because he was mad that Othello, his general had bypassed him to nominate Michael Cassio as his lieutenant and also because he thought Othello was sleeping with his wife, Emilia. Akiaekeme exploited dexterously Adesuwa's naivety just like Iago did with Othello. She will say, "What I just saw; my mouth is too holy to speak." Adesuwa is held captive as she adjures her for the revelations. Akiaekeme will pretend that she doesn't want to hurt her. She will say, "Swear that you will not be hurt." Without waiting for her to finish, Adesuwa will retort, "Are you doubting my womanhood? I swear my mami and even my dead father. I swear my grandparents in the grave." Then she extended her little finger to add impetus.

Akiaekeme (is a Benin name that means "go on and wait for me") began narrating but suddenly stopped en media res. Then she resumed speaking and stopped again mid-way. She said "Adesuwa, don't worry, you will see it yourself. I don't want to be the want who destroyed your marriage." Adesuwa became more agitated and curious. Akiaekeme finally told her a concocted canard which could be sustained from the suspicion she had built. "It is all over the town that your husband, Tom is sleeping with Vera, your cousin. Yes, your Vera of all people." Now Adesuwa wants to explode. That is the Iago syndrome I told you before. Beware!

Thenceforth, Adesuwa is her slave. She will control and manipulate her as she wants. I told Adesuwa that even if she caught them flagrantly, she must know one thing; love conquers all. She must weigh the goodness from her husband and the evil he just committed and then decide which one weighs more. Do not tell me your relationship was hinged on a one time error.

Jealous people are quick to judge and condemn even when the body of evidence is all lies.

If infidelity actually occurred, one must learn to forgive and not bring it back when they are angry. The righteous easily forgive; the sinners easily condemn and judge. Jesus taught us that lesson when they brought to him in an open show a woman caught in adultery. He asked them for the sinless people to lapidate her first. From her greatest accusers to the least, they all absconded. It is not like you do not have alternatives; you can either divorce or stay, but you should forgive.

I told Adesuwa that the third phase is to find out why her husband looked for sex outside. Is it that he did not have enough sex at home or just that she made the place like a war zone that even with the sex, he did not feel love, accepted and valued. Or perhaps she was acting like a porcupine; piercing him with her goads that he could not even come around her for the sex. Was it that he had lost interest in her physical beauty because he married her as a tadpole, but she became like a sow. Therefore, Adesuwa, you must remember where you have fallen. Notwithstanding, I am aware that some men will still be unfaithful no matter what because some allow their sinful nature to overrun them. Nevertheless, at the same time, we know that love conquers all.

Who do you think Adesuwa listened to? She listened to Akiaekeme the village gossiper! Within a short time, she had made Adesuwa a spinster just as she was. Adesuwa lost her home for listening to all those single women like Akiaekeme who deceived her to ruin her marriage because they wanted single company. They appeared happy without but within they were like gall. Ade, (as she was popularly known) should have remembered the Iago Syndrome. Even if you do not like someone 100%, if you put 100% to like them, you too will soon be inseparable. I only hope Adesuwa's case has taught us about the Iago Syndrome.

Until then, beware of Iago Syndrome!

# Chapter Twenty-One

# Limpopo Kratisa

Limpopo lived with his wife of 40 years and 12 kids in Likomba where he will die on July 22, 1986 at 12.00 P.M. He was from a little remote village called Bachuo Ntai (although he was enlightened as if he came from the city of Ntenako). He had lived in Malabo for years. The first three months of his arrival, he was the boulevardier. In those days, Malabo was to Southern Cameroonians as New York is to Africans today. Everyone dreamed of going there, and God had made it possible for Ta Enowfukang. He had taken a nom de guerre or name of adventure: Limpopo Kratisa. Everyone knew he was loaded not only as he came with twelve kids from the same wife, but he also had brought the proceeds of oil money. His long stay abroad had made him to lose touch with his village. Some hated him, but others loved him. He was always a dividing topic amongst those who knew him. I heard of him too when I was a kid. He had seven daughters. As you know, if the palm tree does not get ripe, birds do not hover on it. Every village or city bird always stopped on Limpopo's roof. Unfortunately, Limpopo became sick briefly and died just like a chicken attacked by the Newcastle Disease.

Before Limpopo died, he gave his will. The first was that he should never be put on the cargo area of the car. He wanted his coffin to be inside the van or bus with people. Secondly, he wanted to be buried in Likomba. Thirdly, he had willed everything to his wife. Fourthly, he cautioned the relatives and villagers against shaving his wife's head as she has been shaved already putting up with him for 40 years and above. The night before he died, he gathered his wife and all twelve kids towards his sick bed and told them this will.

Immediately after he died, his older son informed his uncle who convened other relatives living in Douala, Yaoundé, Limbe, Muea, Ekona, and even those who worked in the Tole Tea Plantations. They all assembled. They decided to take him home, but the wife and kids rejected and stated his will. The family head said Limpopo was like a chief, so he will not be buried outside no matter what he told them all, so they ignored his will.

The wake was arranged, and the next day they had rented a 19 seater bus to take him to his village in Bachuo Ntai. They took the coffin and place it on the cargo spot on top of the bus because someone people did not want to sit with a coffin in the bus. Without going 50 kilometers, Limpopo's coffin slipped and fell by the road side. The people took it and retied it back up, this time with stronger ropes. Then after about 100 kilometers, the coffin fell off the car again, this time with Limpopo's corpse out of the coffin smiling. When one old woman saw it, she went into the bush, cut a whip and began whipping Limpopo's corpse. Americans will say "abuse of a dead body." People were praising her " ngore nkwoh (woman tiger), mgbokondem (princess), ngoreh papa (papa's wife), and tamfang (thorny tree)." The corpse became red. They retied the corpse back on top of the bus and as they went 25 miles, the coffin began shaking and shaking, and the driver veered into the bush into a little creek where 12 of the people died.

A timber truck that was coming from Mamfe towed the survivors out of the bush. They took his corpse from the cargo place and put it inside the buss and then made a U Turn back to Likomba where he was buried. The same day that he was buried, he appeared to his sister and told her that he speared their life because they were not in accordance with the rest else they too would have gone. He told her that he was going back to Malabo and will write them. That night, like a spirit leopard that visited a village, Limpopo disappeared into the thick bush.

Perhaps next time people will learn to respect the dead's will. When someone dies and leaves a will, do not change that will. Some houses have been known to be hunted because someone disobeyed a will. At times some have swindled the dead man's will and calamity upon calamity had befallen them.

Until then, do not alter people's wills.

# INDEX OF BIBLE WORDS

## INDEX OF NAMES

www.ingramcontent.com/pod-product-compliance
Lightning Source LLC
Chambersburg PA
CBHW070539130626
46555CB00003B/1498